U.S. Department of Justice
Office of Justice Programs
National Institute of Justice

MW01292104

Death Investigation:
A Guide for the Scene Investigator

Every Scene.
Every Time.

Research Report

U.S. Department of Justice
Office of Justice Programs
810 Seventh Street N.W.
Washington, DC 20531

Janet Reno
Attorney General

Daniel Marcus
Acting Associate Attorney General

Laurie Robinson
Assistant Attorney General

Noël Brennan
Deputy Assistant Attorney General

Jeremy Travis
Director, National Institute of Justice

Department of Justice Response Center:
800–421–6770

Office of Justice Programs
World Wide Web Site:
http://www.ojp.usdoj.gov

National Institute of Justice
World Wide Web Site:
http://www.ojp.usdoj.gov/nij

Death Investigation:
A Guide for the Scene Investigator

Developed and Approved by the
National Medicolegal Review Panel

Executive Director
Steven C. Clark, Ph.D.
Occupational Research and Assessment, Inc.
Big Rapids, Michigan
Associate Professor
Ferris State University

November 1999

The title of this report, formerly "National Guidelines for Death
Investigation," has been changed in this reprint for consistency with
the titles of other Guides in the NIJ series.

U.S. Department of Justice
Office of Justice Programs

National Institute of Justice
Jeremy Travis, J.D.
Director

Richard M. Rau, Ph.D.
Project Monitor

This project was cosponsored by the Centers for Disease Control and Prevention and the Bureau of Justice Assistance.

"Every Scene, Every Time" logo designed and created by Steven Clark, Ph.D., and Kevin Spicer of Occupational Research and Assessment, Inc.

This project was supported under grant number 96–MU–CS–0005 by the National Institute of Justice, Office of Justice Programs, U.S. Department of Justice, and by the Bureau of Justice Assistance and the Centers for Disease Control and Prevention.

NCJ 167568

The National Institute of Justice is a component of the Office of Justice Programs, which also includes the Bureau of Justice Assistance, the Bureau of Justice Statistics, the Office of Juvenile Justice and Delinquency Prevention, and the Office for Victims of Crime.

Message From the Attorney General

The sudden or unexplained death of an individual has a profound impact on families and friends of the deceased and places significant responsibility on the agencies tasked with determining the cause of death. Increasingly, science and technology play a key role in death investigations. One of the hallmarks of science is adherence to clear and well-grounded protocols.

In many jurisdictions, responsibility for conducting death investigations may rest with pathologists, medical examiners, or coroners, in addition to their other duties. There is little training available in the best procedures for handling these crucial and sensitive tasks. To help fill the gap, the National Institute of Justice, joined by the Centers for Disease Control and Prevention and the Bureau of Justice Assistance, supported the development of the guidelines presented in this report.

These guidelines were produced with the vigorous participation of highly experienced officials and professionals who served on the National Medicolegal Review Panel. A technical working group of 144 professionals from across the country provided the grassroots input to the panel's work. I applaud their willingness to take the time to serve in this effort and to hammer out this consensus on the best approach to conducting thorough and competent death investigations.

Jurisdictions will want to carefully consider these guidelines and their applicability to local agencies and circumstances. By adhering to agreed-upon national standards, death investigators can arrive at the truth about a suspicious death. Families and friends can be consoled by knowing what happened to their loved one, and justice can be administered on the foundation of truth that must always guide our work.

Janet Reno
Attorney General

National Medicolegal Review Panel

The National Medicolegal Review Panel (NMRP) represents a multidisciplinary group of content area experts, each representing members of his or her respective organization. Each organization has a role—be it active involvement or oversight—in conducting death investigations and in implementing these guidelines.

United States Conference of Mayors
The Honorable Scott L. King (Chairman, NMRP)
Mayor
Gary, Indiana

American Academy of Forensic Sciences
Joseph H. Davis, M.D.
Retired Director, Dade County Medical Examiner Department
Miami, Florida

American Bar Association
Bruce H. Hanley, Esq.
Partner, Hanley & Dejoras, P.A.
Minneapolis, Minnesota

American Medical Association
Mary E. S. Case, M.D.
Chief Medical Examiner
St. Louis, St. Charles, Jefferson, and Franklin Counties, Missouri
St. Louis University School of Medicine

College of American Pathologists
Jeffrey M. Jentzen, M.D.
Medical Examiner
Milwaukee, Wisconsin

International Association of Chiefs of Police
Chief Thomas J. O'Loughlin
Wellesley, Massachusetts

International Association of Coroners and Medical Examiners
Halbert E. Fillinger, Jr., M.D.
Coroner
Montgomery County, Pennsylvania

National Association of Counties
Douglas A. Mack, M.D., M.P.H.
Chief Medical Examiner and Public Health Director
Kent County, Michigan

National Association of Medical Examiners
Richard C. Harruff, M.D., Ph.D.
Associate Medical Examiner
Seattle/King County Department of Public Health
Seattle, Washington

National Conference of State Legislatures
Representative Jeanne M. Adkins
Colorado State Legislature
House Judiciary Committee
Denver, Colorado

National Governors' Association
Richard T. Callery, M.D., F.C.A.P.
Chief Medical Examiner
Wilmington, Delaware

National Sheriffs' Association
Donald L. Mauro
Commanding Officer, Homicide Bureau
Los Angeles County Sheriff's Department
Los Angeles, California

Colorado Coroners' Association
Elaine R. Meisner
Logan County Coroner
Sterling, Colorado

South Dakota Funeral Directors' Association
George H. Kuhler
Elected Coroner
Beadle County, South Dakota

Acknowledgments

T he author wishes to thank the Technical Working Group for Death Investigation (TWGDI). This 144-member reviewer network gave of their time to review guideline content, providing the researcher feedback from a national perspective. Additional thanks to the TWGDI executive board: Mr. Paul Davison, Kent County M.E. Office, Grand Rapids, Michigan; Mr. Bill Donovan, Jefferson Parish Coroner's Office, Harvey, Louisiana; Mr. Cullen Ellingburgh, Forensic Science Center, Orange County, California; Ms. Roberta Geiselhart, R.N., Hennepin County M.E. Office, Minneapolis, Minnesota; Dr. Elizabeth Kinnison, Office of the Chief M.E., Norfolk, Virginia; Mr. Vernon McCarty, Washoe County Coroner, Reno, Nevada; Mr. Joseph Morgan, Fulton County M.E. Office, Atlanta, Georgia; Mr. Randy Moshos, M.E. Office, New York, New York; Mr. Steve Nunez, Office of the Medical Investigator, Albuquerque, New Mexico; Ms. Rose Marie Psara, R.N., St. Louis County M.E. Office, St. Louis, Missouri; and Mr. Michael Stewart, Denver City and County Coroner's Office, Denver, Colorado, whose combined commitment to the field of death investigation is a tribute to the quality of this document. In addition, the offices that employ each member of the group share in this endeavor. Through their support, each member was given the flexibility they needed to support the project.

The author also wishes to thank the National Institute of Justice's (NIJ's) technical advisors: John E. Smialek, M.D., Chief Medical Examiner, State of Maryland; Randy L. Hanzlick, M.D., Centers for Disease Control and Prevention (CDC) and Emory University School of Medicine; Ms. Mary Fran Ernst, Director of Medicolegal Education, St. Louis University Medical School; and Ms. Mary Lou Kearns, Coroner, Kane County, Illinois. Each made significant contributions to the project's inception, eventual funding, and timely completion. Their dedication to the science of death investigation and to the members of the investigative community is apparent throughout this document.

The Director of NIJ, the Honorable Jeremy Travis; the Director of NIJ's Office of Science and Technology, Mr. David G. Boyd; and NIJ's Forensic Science Program Manager, Richard M. Rau, Ph.D., each share responsibility for the success of this project. Credit also goes to R. Gib Parrish, M.D., of CDC, for his support and commitment to the research.

In addition, the true strength of these guidelines is derived from the stamina of the National Medicolegal Review Panel, whose members represented 12 national organizations intimately involved in the investigation of death and its outcomes. The panel also included two representatives of elected coroners. NMRP's contribution was invaluable.

And finally, the leadership of Joseph H. Davis, M.D., Medical Examiner Emeritus, Dade County, Florida, and Mr. Donald Murray, National Association of Counties, for their unrelenting efforts to get this job done and improve their profession, every scene, every time.

Steven C. Clark, Ph.D.
Executive Director

Contents

Foreword: Commentaries on the Need for Guidelines for Death Investigation

_____ Commentary _____

Jeanne M. Adkins
Representative
State Legislature, Colorado

Few things in our democracy are as important as ensuring that citizens have confidence in their institutions in a crisis. For many individuals the death of a loved one is just such a crisis. Ensuring that the proper steps and procedures are taken at the scene of that death to reassure family members that the death was a natural one, a suicide, or a homicide is a key element in maintaining citizen confidence in local officials.

How local death investigators do their job is crucial to family members who are mourning a loss today and who may be seeking justice tomorrow. Most of us cringe at the idea of death investigations where important steps were omitted that might have led to arrests and ultimately convictions in those deaths. Justice denied breeds contempt for the institutions created to ensure that justice is done.

It is with such thoughts in mind that I encourage State legislators to focus some attention on this issue and look at adopting model legislation that establishes death investigation procedures and encourages all local jurisdictions to spend some resources training those on the front lines to follow those procedures. Success in this national effort depends on the initiative of State legislators to take the first steps by making this a priority.

_____ Commentary _____

Richard T. Callery, M.D., F.C.A.P.
Chief Medical Examiner
Director, Forensic Sciences Laboratory
Wilmington, Delaware

As the representative of the National Governors' Association, I am honored to have been chosen to participate in the National Medicolegal Review Panel. The hard work and commitment by the panel resulted in guidelines that are long overdue for setting the standard of practice for death investigation of "other than natural" cases. We are all acutely aware of the ramifications of our proposed national guidelines. Each death, especially those other than natural, has a profound impact on society, particularly the criminal justice system. Standardization nationwide is long overdue. This panel can take pride in producing a work product of such high quality that will assist in establishing a standard of practice for death investigation in the United States.

_____ Commentary _____

Mary E. S. Case, M.D.
Chief Medical Examiner
St. Louis, St. Charles, Jefferson, and
Franklin Counties, Missouri

As the representative member from the American Medical Association serving on the National Medicolegal Review Panel, I have had the opportunity to observe and become familiar with the development of the *Death Investigation: A Guide for the Scene Investigator.* I am delighted with this effort and enthusiastically support and endorse the guidelines that have been developed.

As a faculty member at St. Louis University Health Sciences Center in the Division of Forensic Pathology, I have been part of our Medicolegal Death Investigators Course since its inception in 1978. I am aware of the tremendous importance of medicolegal death investigation in the proper administration of justice and criminal proceedings, adjudicating estates, and handling of death certification; and, unfortunately, I am aware of the all too common poor level at which some jurisdictions function in death investigation.

One of the most certain methods of ensuring uniform and proper procedural compliance in death investigation is to establish guidelines that can be followed in every instance. A good example of the use of guidelines in death investigation is the death investigation of an infant, for which many jurisdictions have established a protocol for conducting the scene investigation. By definition, a diagnosis of Sudden Infant Death Syndrome (SIDS) can be made only after the scene investigation, autopsy, microscopic, toxicology, and medical history have been conducted, and all have been unrevealing as to a cause of death.

The first step toward uniform excellence in death investigation is to establish guidelines that can be followed by even those jurisdictions having minimal resources. The efforts of the National Medicolegal Death Investigation Guidelines Project to create a structured protocol for the necessary tasks to be accomplished at death scenes have been highly successful in fulfilling that goal.

Commentary

Joseph H. Davis, M.D.
Retired Director, Dade County
Medical Examiner Department
Professor of Pathology Emeritus,
University of Miami

The objectives of the American Academy of Forensic Sciences are enunciated in the Preamble of its Bylaws and include: "to improve the practice, elevate the standards and advance the cause of the forensic sciences . . . ." *Death Investigation: A Guide for the Scene Investigator* most certainly supports the objectives of the academy when sudden, unexpected, and violent deaths are investigated by forensic pathologists and other scientists. Sudden death investigation is multidisciplinary, with involvement of scientists representing all sections of the academy—pathology, odontology, criminalistics, toxicology, psychiatry, questioned documents, jurisprudence, and even engineering. None of these scientists can be truly effective if the death investigation is faulted by errors of omission or commission during the initial scene investigation.

Eventually, the States of the Union will see the wisdom of uniform quality of standards and training for medicolegal death investigators. However, such standards are impossible unless consensus is reached as to what subjects should be taught and how investigators should be judged as to entry and performance in the field of death investigation. These guidelines are the first step for the eventual implementation of proper standards and training throughout the United States.

Commentary

Halbert E. Fillinger, Jr., M.D.
Forensic Pathologist
Coroner
Montgomery County, Pennsylvania

I have been honored to represent the International Association of Coroners and Medical Examiners on the National Medicolegal Review Panel. The end product of the efforts of this panel in developing universal guidelines for death-scene investigation fills a long-vacant gap in the training and investigation of sudden, suspicious death.

It has been apparent to me in my 40 years of experience as a forensic pathologist, assistant medical examiner and coroner, as well as death-scene investigation trainer, that systematic, specific guidelines are essential to good death-scene investigation. The guidelines promulgated by the National Medicolegal Review Panel fill a need that has long been recognized by most of our colleagues in the field, and this can only greatly enhance and improve the quality of our work.

With many of the deaths today having more and more civil as well as criminal implications, top-quality death-scene investigation becomes a must in any jurisdiction, and I feel that the product of the National Medicolegal Review Panel will fill this need.

I am incorporating the guidelines developed thus far in the mandatory training program for the Commonwealth of Pennsylvania as directed by the Attorney General's Office, and find that the guidelines are well structured and comprehensive, yet simple to follow. One can systematically start with an experienced investigator or a very inexperienced one and, by following these guidelines, a competent quality death-scene investigation can be carried out.

Without the efforts of the National Medicolegal Review Panel, no systematic, universal, top-quality investigation can be expected with the diverse backgrounds of the coroners and medical examiners in the United States.

Commentary

Bruce H. Hanley, Esq.
Partner, Hanley & Dejoras, P.A.
Minneapolis, Minnesota

The development of *Death Investigation: A Guide for the Scene Investigator* will be of great benefit to all citizens. The guidelines will help to promote consistency, accuracy, predictability, and reliability in death-scene investigations. As a criminal defense lawyer, it is a chief concern that a person is not wrongfully accused of having participated in a homicide. Complete, thorough, and careful death-scene investigations can lead to greater faith in the system by family and friends of those whose deaths may have been caused by homicide, suicide, accident, or natural causes. Elimination of unanswered questions, confusion, sloppiness, and the lack of attention to detail all can contribute to the genuine acceptance that the cause of death has been properly determined. Moreover, in the case of homicide, all can have a strong belief in the accuracy of the identification of the perpetrator. The guidelines will assist the actual investigators in following the proper protocol and consistently obtaining all available evidence to show that the death was the result of either unlawful or lawful activity. Proper adherence to the guidelines, coupled with proper training to implement the guidelines, will serve to satisfy finders of fact in criminal cases that the State has presented accurate, reliable, and trustworthy evidence. Additionally, it will serve to defuse attacks by defense counsel on the investigative methods and techniques, chain of custody, and the reliability of any testing that may have been conducted during the course of the investigation. It may also serve to prevent innocent people from being accused of criminal activity when, in fact, a crime was not committed, or the person suspected was not involved. The truth is the outcome sought, and the guidelines will assist the system in obtaining the truth. In a criminal investigation, when the government follows the rules and properly conducts its investigation, it will win most of the time. When it does not follow the rules or properly conduct its investigation, it should lose.

Commentary

Randy Hanzlick, M.D.
Centers for Disease Control and Prevention
Atlanta, Georgia

Variations in statutes, levels of funding, geography and population density, and death investigator education, training, and experience result in variations in the quality and extent of medicolegal death investigations. Front-line, on-scene death investigations are performed by people whose jobs range from part-time to full-time, and whose education, training, and experience vary substantially and range from minimal to extensive. The outcome of death investigations may impact personal liberty and well-being, adjudication of cases, public health and safety, mortality statistics, research capabilities, and governmental approaches to legislation and programs. Therefore, high-quality death investigation throughout the United States is a desirable goal for many reasons.

The creation of guidelines for medicolegal death investigations is one method of promoting uniformity in the approach to death investigations and improving or assuring their quality at the same time. Guidelines may also be used as a basis for developing educational programs, to evaluate work performance, and as a basis for credentialing or certification of death investigators. To those ends, the National Medicolegal Review Panel has taken an important step by developing this initial set of death investigation guidelines as a model for nationwide use, pursuant to a grant funded by the National Institute of Justice and the Centers for Disease Control and Prevention.

The development of such guidelines will not be enough in and of themselves, however. The best intended and designed guidelines will have little effect if death investigators are not provided with funds adequate to meet the provisions of the guidelines. Funding for the education and training of death investigation practices and for the implementation of the guidelines will be necessary, and funding needs pose a significant obstacle to the long-term goal of nationwide improvement in death investigation practices. Governments at every level of organization will need to explore methods for acquiring or providing funds and providing the education, training, and manpower to effectively implement these and any subsequent guidelines. In the meantime, these guidelines provide a starting point from which we can proceed.

Commentary

Richard C. Harruff, M.D., Ph.D.
Associate Medical Examiner
Seattle/King County
Department of Public Health
Seattle, Washington

A competent and thorough death-scene investigation provides the basis for a comprehensive medicolegal autopsy, and together the scene investigation and autopsy provide the basis for an accurate determination of cause and manner of death. Furthermore, following specific guidelines helps assure that all relevant aspects of all deaths are fully investigated. Representing the National Association of Medical Examiners on the National Medicolegal Review Panel, I believe that the national guidelines for death-scene investigation offer medical examiners and coroners a valuable means for substantially enhancing performance in fulfilling their far-ranging responsibilities. As the guidelines have been formulated with the consensus of several prominent forensic and legal experts, they represent a major advancement in scientific death investigation and deserve the attention of all who claim competency in this field.

Commentary

Jeffrey M. Jentzen, M.D.
Medical Examiner
Milwaukee County, Wisconsin

As a member of the Forensic Pathology Committee of the College of American Pathologists, I would like to encourage my colleagues to consider the impact that national guidelines would have on the investigation of sudden and unexpected deaths. Most pathologists assist law enforcement officials in medicolegal death investigations during their careers in some form or another. We are aware that an investigation requires the proper coordination of a number of agencies and that the breakdown of the investigative procedures may jeopardize the successful outcome of the case. *Death Investigation: A Guide for the Scene Investigator* provides procedures for uniform death-scene processing, which ensures competent and complete examination of the death scene in a judicious manner that also respects the concerns of the family and loved ones. The guidelines set forth in this document have been developed by a diverse panel of professional death investigators who understand the common pitfalls of everyday medicolegal death investigation. Medicolegal death investigation has become a sophisticated process subject to critical review and high expectations of the community, the legal system, and family members. These guidelines provide the essential tasks for death-scene investigation and go a long way toward ensuring quality death-scene investigations.

Commentary

Mary Lou Kearns, R.N., M.P.H.
Coroner
Kane County, Illinois

Historically, the Office of Coroner has been charged with the responsibilities and duties of answering pertinent questions related to death investigation: Who, What, When, Where, How, and Why. Only when these questions have been answered correctly can all the proper legal issues that arise at death be handled expertly and completely for the administration of justice. As the representative of the coroners of America on the NIJ Peer Review Panel, I applaud the efforts that have produced *Death Investigation: A Guide for the Scene Investigator.* These guidelines provide the necessary policies and procedures for universal and professional death-scene investigations, as well as the criteria for when to be suspicious. And by having properly coordinated death-scene investigative procedures, the community, the legal system, and family members will be well served.

I have long been committed to this quest for universal guidelines and the eventual training of death investigators nationwide. Coroners who are well trained in their jobs make fewer mistakes. The more training and confidence coroners have, the better our offices will run. An ideal coroner's office is well prepared to investigate and evaluate a scene, to examine a body, to write quality reports, and to interact with the family, all in a professional manner. These national guidelines for death-scene investigations will go a long way toward enhancing our professionalism.

———————————— Commentary ————————

Mayor Scott L. King, Chairman, NMRP
Mayor
Gary, Indiana

As the representative of the United States Conference of Mayors, I was pleased to serve as Chairman of the National Medicolegal Review Panel, particularly given the expertise and wide range of diverse experience of the balance of the panel. Because the duties of a mayor include responsibility for public safety functions, and because I served for 20 years as both a prosecution and defense attorney before assuming my present office, I am acutely aware of the importance of establishing and utilizing appropriate protocol for death-scene investigations. These guidelines will, I hope, accomplish the goal of uniformity in the conduct of such investigations nationwide without requiring significant additional expenditure of budget funds.

———————————— Commentary ————————

George H. Kuhler
Elected Coroner
Beadle County, South Dakota

I would like to encourage all elected coroners to consider supporting national guidelines for coroner investigations. As a funeral director and elected coroner, I know firsthand how important proper investigation is to the law enforcement community, as well as to the forensic medical/legal investigation of the death. With no "official training" required for elected coroners, it is difficult for the elected coroner to know what should be done in investigations. Most elected coroners have begun their jobs with little or no knowledge as to how and what they need to do. Having a set of national guidelines for medicolegal death investigation would ensure that at least the elected coroner would have a "cookbook" to follow and would have some idea of what is expected of him/her in every case.

I would encourage the adoption and use of the following guidelines for all coroners, medical examiners, and death investigators. These guidelines have been developed by a panel of members from all of these fields from across the United States. The use of these guidelines on every scene will ensure quality and uniform death investigation every time.

Commentary

Douglas A. Mack, M.D., M.P.H.
Chief Medical Examiner and
Public Health Director
Kent County, Michigan

As a representative of the National Association of Counties and as Chief Medical Examiner for Kent County, Michigan, I enthusiastically endorse the medicolegal guidelines developed by the National Medicolegal Review Panel for death-scene investigation and medical examiner system processes. An efficient, well-managed, and high-quality medical examiner system is a critical element in death investigation and benefits the law enforcement, criminal justice, and public health systems. This protocol provides direction for the interaction of these systems, and helps assure that the work of those involved results in high-quality investigations and outcomes.

Commentary

Donald L. Mauro
Commanding Officer, Homicide Bureau
Los Angeles County Sheriff's Department
Los Angeles, California

As a representative of the National Sheriffs' Association, I have been honored to participate with the very capable and diverse group that comprises the National Medicolegal Review Panel. The results of our efforts are the national guidelines, which will direct the efforts of fellow death investigators in "other than natural" death investigations. The procedures developed by the panel constitute a baseline protocol that should serve to support and direct the efforts of all of us who work in this field. Because each death has profound implications for family and friends, and because each investigation ultimately has financial, legal, and societal implications, we can take satisfaction in knowing that standards now exist for death investigators across the country, which, when followed, will yield comprehensive, high-quality death-scene investigations.

Commentary

Elaine R. Meisner
Logan County Coroner
Sterling, Colorado

As a member of the Colorado Coroners' Association, it is with a great deal of pride and sense of accomplishment that I have been their representative on the National Medicolegal Review Panel for death investigation guidelines. In the rural areas, the importance and necessity of thorough and proper death investigations have not always been thought of as an area of much importance, not so much by the agencies doing the investigations, but by the agencies who financially support them. As a lifelong resident of a rural community, I value and appreciate the importance and need of a thorough and proper death investigation. These guidelines have been long awaited by many death investigators across the country. The National Medicolegal Review Panel has worked hard to develop a sound, well-described set of death investigation guidelines. Today, the modern range of knowledge is much greater, techniques are precise and specialized. These methodically well-planned guidelines were much needed to ensure and maintain uniformity and to help decrease chance for error. This has been a unique experience with the display of utmost professionalism and collaboration by committee members. Without the unstinting cooperation and help of all concerned, it would have been impossible to finish this project. It is in the best interests of death investigators nationwide to utilize these appropriately developed guidelines for the purpose of improving death investigations and for other agencies to properly support them.

Thomas J. O'Loughlin
Chief of Police
Wellesley, Massachusetts

The proposed *Death Investigation: A Guide for the Scene Investigator* has been developed with the input of members of the various and many disciplines that are involved in the investigation of sudden and unexpected deaths.

The investigation of the death of another human being is a weighty responsibility. It has been a pleasure to represent and serve the interests of the International Association of Chiefs of Police in participating in the development of *Death Investigation: A Guide for the Scene Investigator.*

As a police officer and chief of police, I am well aware of the multifaceted and multidisciplinary approach that is necessary in many of these investigations. As professionals, we are all aware of investigations that have been met with professional success and those that have been, unfortunately, less than professional.

As important as the actual performance of the investigative procedures is an understanding of the diverse and mutual responsibilities held by involved and participating professionals. *Death Investigation: A Guide for the Scene Investigator* will provide standardized procedures so that each and every participant in the death-scene investigation will have a clear and concise understanding of the professionally accepted standards and procedures necessary in conducting a death-scene investigation.

In the long term, it is the expected goal that each of the participants within the death investigation process will meet these established professional standards and their obligation to fulfill their responsibilities in a competent and professional manner.

Commentary

John E. Smialek, M.D.
Chief Medical Examiner
State of Maryland

A major step in the advancement of the American system of justice was taken recently with the recognition of standard guidelines for scene investigation in medical examiner and coroner cases.

Awareness of inadequate death investigation operations in jurisdictions around the country resulted in a project supported by the National Institute of Justice that has produced the new guidelines.

The panel of experts assembled by NIJ considered the need for standards that were comprehensive but flexible and capable of being adapted to operations that utilize a variety of investigative officials including police officers, sheriffs, justices of the peace, physicians, and pathologists.

Further progress in achieving a system of death investigation that meets the needs of law enforcement agencies and families will depend on the willingness of State and local government officials to support the introduction of these guidelines and provide the necessary resources to implement them.

As a representative of the National Association of Medical Examiners, I strongly urge the careful study and acceptance of these standards.

Introduction

"Is it [death investigation] an enlightened system? No, it's not. It's really no better than what they have in many Third World countries."

Dr. Werner Spitz, Former Chief Medical Examiner, Wayne County (Detroit), Michigan

The first thing one must realize is that the word "system" is a misnomer, when used in the context of death investigation in the United States. There is no "system" of death investigation that covers the more than 3,000 jurisdictions in this country.[1] No nationally accepted guidelines or standards of practice exist for individuals responsible for performing death-scene investigations. No professional degree, license, certification, or minimum educational requirements exist, nor is there a commonly accepted training curriculum. Not even a common job title exists for the thousands of people who routinely perform death investigations in this country.[2, 3]

This report describes a study that focused on the establishment of guidelines for conducting death investigations.

Purpose and Scope of the Study

The principal purpose of the study, initiated in June 1996, was to identify, delineate, and assemble a set of investigative tasks that should and could be performed at every death scene. These tasks would serve as the foundation of the guide for death scene investigators. The Director of the National Institute of Justice (NIJ) selected an independent review panel whose members represented international and national organizations whose constituents are responsible for the investigation of death and its outcomes. The researcher organized two multidisciplinary technical working groups (TWGs). The first consisted of members representing the investigative community at large, and the second consisted of an executive board representing the investigative community at large.

The study involved the use of two standardized consensus-seeking research techniques: (a) the **D**eveloping **A** Curricul**UM** (DACUM)[4] process, and (b) a Delphi[5] survey.

In this report, the author does not attempt to assign responsibility for task (guideline) performance to any one occupational job title (e.g., Guideline D4 is performed by law enforcement personnel). Research design and selected methodology focused on the establishment of performance guidelines for death-scene investigations. The research design did not allow TWGs to assume investigative outcomes during the development phase of the project; therefore, no attempt was made to assign a "manner" of death to individual guidelines (e.g., Guideline C2 applies to homicide scenes), to maintain objectivity and national practicality.

The author does not claim to be an expert in the science and/or methodology of medicolegal death investigation. This research was based on the collective knowledge of three multidisciplinary content area expert groups. The focus was on the death scene, the body, and the interactive skills and knowledge that must be applied to ensure a successful case outcome.

The balance of this introduction outlines the study design and provides basic background information on the selection of the National Medicolegal Review Panel (NMRP) and TWG memberships and the research methodology, its selection, and application. The study findings (investigative guidelines) follow this introduction.

Study Design

Identification of NMRP and TWGs

The methodology selected for this occupational research required collection of data from a sample of current subject matter experts, practitioners from the field who perform daily within the occupation being investigated. This "criterion" was used to identify members of the various multidisciplinary groups that provided the data for this research.

The following groups were formed for the purpose of developing national guidelines for conducting death investigations.

National Medicolegal Review Panel

NMRP members represent an independent multidisciplinary group of both international and national organizations whose constituents are responsible for investigating death and its outcomes. Each member of NMRP was selected by the Director based on nominations made by the various associations. The rationale for their involvement was twofold: (a) they represent the diversity of the profession nationally, and (b) their members are the key stakeholders in the outcomes of this research. Each organization has a role in conducting death investigations and in implementing these guidelines.

Technical Working Group for Death Investigation (TWGDI)

1. National Reviewer Network

Technical Working Group for Death Investigation (TWGDI) members represent a sample of death investigators from across the country. They are the content area experts who perform within the occupation daily. The following criteria were used to select the members of the TWGDI reviewer network:

◆ Each member was nominated/selected for the position by a person whose name appeared on the most recent (1995) Centers for Disease Control and Prevention (CDC) national database of death investigation.[6]

◆ Each member had specific knowledge regarding the investigation of death.

◆ Each member had specific experience with the process of death investigation and the outcomes of positive and negative scene investigations.

◆ Each member could commit to four rounds of national surveying over a 6-month period.

A 50-percent random sample (1,512) of death investigators was drawn from the Centers for Disease Control and Prevention database.[7] A letter was sent to each member of the sample, inviting him or her to participate in the national research to develop death investigative guidelines or to nominate a person who participates in death investigations. Two hundred and sixty-three individuals were nominated (17 percent). Nominees were contacted by mail and asked to provide personal demographic data including job title, years of experience, and educational background, in addition to general information (name/address, etc.) necessary for participation in the research.

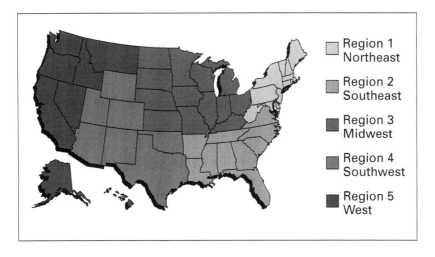

The TWGDI national reviewer network consisted of 263 members from 46 States, representing 5 regions as follows:

Region	Location	Number of Participants	Percentage
1	Northeast	32	12.2%
2	Southeast	56	21.3%
3	Midwest	94	35.7%
4	Southwest	47	17.9%
5	West	34	12.9%

The educational backgrounds of the national reviewer network members were as follows:

Education	Number	Percentage
Law Enforcement	82	31.2%
Medical	157	59.8%
Unknown	24	9.0%

The types of investigative systems represented on the reviewer network were as follows:

System	Number	Percentage
Medical Examiner	44	16.6%
Coroner	161	61.3%
Mixed ME/Coroner	58	22.1%

The average age of TWGDI members was 47.6 years. They had an average of 10.5 years of experience. There were 80.6 percent (212) males and 19.4 percent (51) females in the group.

2. Executive Board

Representatives from each region were selected to maintain consistency within regions across the United States. These representatives made up the TWGDI executive board.

Criteria for selection to the TWGDI executive board were as follows:

◆ Each member had specific knowledge regarding the investigation of death.

◆ Each member had specific experience with the process of death investigation and the outcomes of positive and negative scene investigations.

◆ Each member could commit to attend four workshops held within the grant period.

TWGDI Executive Board DACUM Workshop. In November 1996, the TWGDI executive board met in St. Louis to begin developing the national Delphi survey. The survey content was to reflect "best practice" for death-scene investigation. DACUM is a process for analyzing an occupation systematically. The 2-day workshop used the investigative experts on the executive board to analyze job tasks while employing modified brainstorming techniques. The board's efforts resulted in a DACUM chart that describes the investigative occupation in terms of specific tasks that competent investigators must be able to perform "every scene, every time."[8] A task was defined as a unit of observable work with a specific beginning and ending point that leads to an investigative product, service, or decision. The DACUM chart served as the outline for the Delphi survey.

This initial process resulted in six major areas of work. In attempts to simplify the survey for the members of the national reviewer network, the areas of work were placed into a logical sequence of events (as they might be performed while investigating a case). Within the five major areas of work (Investigative Tools and Equipment was excluded at this point because tools and equipment are "things," not procedural steps), 29 tasks were identified. Within the 29 identified investigative tasks were 149 discrete steps and/or elements. Theoretically, each step and/or element must be performed for the task to be completed "successfully." The results were placed in survey format for NMRP review and pilot testing.

National Medicolegal Review Panel Meeting. In December 1996, NMRP met in Washington, D.C., to review the DACUM chart and comment on the research methodology proposed by the researcher. The members of the panel recommended modifications to the survey design and approved response selections. Respondents would attempt to rate, by perceived importance, each of the investigative tasks/steps and/or elements on a five-point scale.

The Delphi Survey. The Delphi technique, although it employs questionnaires, is much different from the typical questionnaire survey. Developed by the RAND Corporation as a method of predicting future defense needs, the technique is used whenever a consensus is needed from persons who are knowledgeable about a particular subject.[9] The goal of a Delphi survey is to engage the respondents in an anonymous debate in order to arrive at consensus on particular issues or on predictions of future events.

The Delphi requires at least four rounds in an effort to obtain a well-thought-out consensus. After the first-round results were received, coded, and recorded, a revised questionnaire was developed for round two. The second-round survey provided each member of TWGDI with the national median and mean scores for each of the task statements presented, as well as their first-round responses. Respondents were asked to compare their original ratings with the median and mean scores and to revise their original evaluations as they saw fit. This procedure was repeated for each of the four rounds of the survey.

The Delphi survey was conducted during the first 6 months of 1997. The table below provides general TWGDI response data:

Round	Surveys Sent	Surveys Received	Cumulative Respondent Loss (%)
1	263	199	24.3%
2	199	163	13.72%
3	163	149	5.33%
4	149	146	1.14%

As shown in the preceding table, final membership in the TWGDI national reviewer network was 146. This number represents approximately 56 percent of the originally nominated members.

Guideline Development. During the 6 months of the Delphi process, both the TWGDI executive board and NMRP met to review survey data (to date) and to begin the process of moving task-based data into guideline format.

In May 1997, the executive board met for a 2 1/2-day working session in New Orleans to begin the guideline development process. The consensus of the board was to establish 29 guidelines based on the national reviewer network data and present them to NMRP for review. Each guideline would have the following content:

◆ A statement of *principle,* citing the rationale for performing the guideline.

◆ A statement of *authorization,* citing specific policy empowering the investigator.

◆ A statement of *policy* to the investigator regarding guideline performance.

◆ The *procedure* for performing the guideline.

◆ A statement of *summary,* citing justification for performing the procedures.

In June and July 1997, NMRP met for two 1 1/2-day working sessions in St. Louis and Chicago to review the draft guidelines developed by the executive board and offer recommendations and changes based on jurisdictional variances and organizational responsibilities. Those sessions resulted in the final draft of the 29 guidelines for conducting death investigations. The 29 guidelines are presented in the next main section.

Guideline Status

Currently, NMRP members are presenting the guidelines to their respective organizations' leadership (or appropriate internal committees) for review. This researcher is collecting anecdotal comments for future modification of the existing guidelines during the validation procedures.

Training Guidelines

The purpose of the second part of the national death investigator guidelines research was to identify training criteria for each of the 29 guidelines. This research is now completed. For each of the guidelines presented in this report, "minimum levels of performance" will be developed and verified by the members of the various TWGs. These "training guidelines" will provide both individuals and educational organizations the material needed to establish and maintain valid exit outcomes for each investigative trainee.

Guideline Validation

In this initial research, 29 investigative tasks were identified. Each task was developed into a guideline for investigators to follow while conducting a death investigation. Although each TWG believed in the validity of each guideline, no attempt was made to validate actual significance (e.g., if guideline C1 is trained and implemented, a [%] decrease in poor scene photographs should occur). The researcher is currently developing a national validation strategy for the implementation and validation of each guideline.

Notes

1. "It is important to note that even the use of the word 'system' to describe a process that encompasses more than 3,000 individual jurisdictions is a misnomer." Hansen, M., "Body of Evidence," *American Bar Association Journal* (June 1995).

2. Jentzen, J.M., S.C. Clark, and M.F. Ernst, "Medicolegal Death Investigator Pre-Employment Test Development," *American Journal of Forensic Medicine and Pathology* 17 (1996):112–16.

3. Hanzlick, R., "Coroner Training Needs: A Numeric and Geographic Analysis," *Journal of the American Medical Association* 276 (1996):1775–1778.

4. The Ohio State University, Center on Education and Training for Employment, DACUM, 1996.

5. Borg, W.R., and M.D. Gall, *Educational Research: An Introduction,* New York: Longman Inc., 1983:413–415.

6. Combs, D., R.G. Parrish, and R.T. Ing, *Death Investigation in the United States and Canada,* Atlanta: U.S. Department of Health and Human Services, Public Health Service, Centers for Disease Control and Prevention, 1995.

7. Ibid.

8. Clark, S.C., Occupational Research and Assessment, Inc., Big Rapids, Michigan, 1996.

9. Borg and Gall, 413–415.

Medicolegal Death Investigation Guidelines

Section A	Investigative Tools and Equipment

Section B	Arriving at the Scene

Section C	Documenting and Evaluating the Scene

Section D	Documenting and Evaluating the Body

Section E	Establishing and Recording Decedent Profile Information

Section F	Completing the Scene Investigation

11

Investigative Tools and Equipment

1. Gloves (Universal Precautions).
2. Writing implements (pens, pencils, markers).
3. Body bags.
4. Communication equipment (cell phone, pager, radio).
5. Flashlight.
6. Body ID tags.
7. Camera—35mm (with extra batteries, film, etc.).
8. Investigative notebook (for scene notes, etc.).
9. Measurement instruments (tape measure, ruler, rolling measuring tape, etc.).
10. Official identification (for yourself).
11. Watch.
12. Paper bags (for hands, feet, etc.).
13. Specimen containers (for evidence items and toxicology specimens).
14. Disinfectant (Universal Precautions).
15. Departmental scene forms.
16. Camera—Polaroid (with extra film).
17. Blood collection tubes (syringes and needles).
18. Inventory lists (clothes, drugs, etc.).
19. Paper envelopes.
20. Clean white linen sheet (stored in plastic bag).
21. Evidence tape.
22. Business cards/office cards w/phone numbers.
23. Foul-weather gear (raincoat, umbrella, etc.).
24. Medical equipment kit (scissors, forceps, tweezers, exposure suit, scalpel handle, blades, disposable syringe, large gauge needles, cotton-tipped swabs, etc.).
25. Phone listing (important phone numbers).
26. Tape or rubber bands.
27. Disposable (paper) jumpsuits, hair covers, face shield, etc.
28. Evidence seal (use with body bags/locks).

29. Pocketknife.

30. Shoe-covers.

31. Trace evidence kit (tape, etc.).

32. Waterless hand wash.

33. Thermometer.

34. Crime scene tape.

35. First aid kit.

36. Latent print kit.

37. Local maps.

38. Plastic trash bags.

39. Gunshot residue analysis kits (SEM/EDS).

40. Photo placards (signage to ID case in photo).

41. Boots (for wet conditions, construction sites, etc.).

42. Hand lens (magnifying glass).

43. Portable electric area lighting.

44. Barrier sheeting (to shield body/area from public view).

45. Purification mask (disposable).

46. Reflective vest.

47. Tape recorder.

48. Basic handtools (boltcutter, screwdrivers, hammer, shovel, trowel, paintbrushes, etc.).

49. Body bag locks (to secure body inside bag).

50. Camera—Video (with extra battery).

51. Personal comfort supplies (insect spray, sun screen, hat, etc.).

52. Presumptive blood test kit.

This handbook is intended as a guide to recommended practices for the investigation of death scenes. Jurisdictional, logistical, or legal conditions may preclude the use of particular procedures contained herein.

Arriving at the Scene

1. Introduce and Identify Self and Role

Principle: Introductions at the scene allow the investigator to establish formal contact with other official agency representatives. The investigator must identify the first responder to ascertain if any artifacts or contamination may have been introduced to the death scene. The investigator must work with all key people to ensure scene safety prior to his/her entrance into the scene.

B

Authorization: Medical Examiner/Coroner Official Office Policy Manual; State or Federal Statutory Authority.

Policy: The investigator shall take the initiative to introduce himself or herself, identify essential personnel, establish rapport, and determine scene safety.

Procedure: Upon arrival at the scene, and prior to entering the scene, the investigator should:

A. Identify the lead investigator at the scene and present identification.

B. Identify other essential officials at the scene (e.g., law enforcement, fire, EMS, social/child protective services, etc.) and explain the investigator's role in the investigation.

C. Identify and document the identity of the first essential official(s) to the scene (first "professional" arrival at the scene for investigative followup) to ascertain if any artifacts or contamination may have been introduced to the death scene.

D. Determine the scene safety (prior to entry).

Summary:

Introductions at the scene help to establish a collaborative investigative effort. It is essential to carry identification in the event of questioned authority. It is essential to establish scene safety prior to entry.

2.   Exercise Scene Safety

Principle: Determining scene safety for all investigative personnel is essential to the investigative process. The risk of environmental and physical injury must be removed prior to initiating a scene investigation. Risks can include hostile crowds, collapsing structures, traffic, and environmental and chemical threats.

Authorization: Medical Examiner/Coroner Official Office Policy Manual; State or Federal Statutory Authority.

Policy: The investigator shall attempt to establish scene safety prior to entering the scene to prevent injury or loss of life, including contacting appropriate agencies for assistance with other scene safety issues.

Procedure: Upon arrival at the scene, the investigator should:

A. Assess and/or establish physical boundaries.

B. Identify incident command.

C. Secure vehicle and park as safely as possible.

D. Use personal protective safety devices (physical, biochemical safety).

E. Arrange for removal of animals or secure (if present and possible).

F. Obtain clearance/authorization to enter scene from the individual responsible for scene safety (e.g., fire marshal, disaster coordinator).

G. While exercising scene safety, protect the integrity of the scene and evidence to the extent possible from contamination or loss by people, animals, and elements.

Note: Due to potential scene hazards (e.g., crowd control, collapsing structures, poisonous gases, traffic), the body may have to be removed before scene investigation can be continued.

Summary:

Environmental and physical threats to the investigator must be removed in order to conduct a scene investigation safely. Protective devices must be used by investigative staff to prevent injury. The investigator must endeavor to protect the evidence against contamination or loss.

3. Confirm or Pronounce Death

Principle: Appropriate personnel must make a determination of death prior to the initiation of the death investigation. The confirmation or pronouncement of death determines jurisdictional responsibilities.

Authorization: Medical Examiner/Coroner Official Office Policy Manual; State or Federal Statutory Authority.

Policy: The investigator shall ensure that appropriate personnel have viewed the body and that death has been confirmed.

Procedure: Upon arrival at the scene, the investigator should:

A. Locate and view the body.

B. Check for pulse, respiration, and reflexes, as appropriate.

C. Identify and document the individual who made the official determination of death, including the date and time of determination.

D. Ensure death is pronounced, as required.

3. Confirm or Pronounce Death

Summary:

Once death has been determined, rescue/resuscitative efforts cease and medicolegal jurisdiction can be established. It is vital that this occur prior to the medical examiner/coroner's assuming any responsibilities.

4. Participate in Scene Briefing (With Attending Agency Representatives)

Principle: Scene investigators must recognize the varying jurisdictional and statutory responsibilities that apply to individual agency representatives (e.g., law enforcement, fire, EMT, judicial/legal). Determining each agency's investigative responsibility at the scene is essential in planning the scope and depth of each scene investigation and the release of information to the public.

Authorization: Medical Examiner/Coroner Official Office Policy Manual; State or Federal Statutory Authority.

Policy: The investigator shall identify specific responsibilities, share appropriate preliminary information, and establish investigative goals of each agency present at the scene.

Procedure: When participating in scene briefing, the investigator should:

A. Locate the staging area (entry point to scene, command post, etc.).

B. Document the scene location (address, mile marker, building name) consistent with other agencies.

C. Determine nature and scope of investigation by obtaining preliminary investigative details (e.g., suspicious versus nonsuspicious death).

D. Ensure that initial accounts of incident are obtained from the first witness(es).

Summary:

Scene briefing allows for initial and factual information exchange. This includes scene location, time factors, initial witness information, agency responsibilities, and investigative strategy.

5.   Conduct Scene "Walk Through"

Principle: Conducting a scene "walk through" provides the investigator with an overview of the entire scene. The "walk through" provides the investigator with the first opportunity to locate and view the body, identify valuable and/or fragile evidence, and determine initial investigative procedures providing for a systematic examination and documentation of the scene and body.

Authorization: Medical Examiner/Coroner Official Office Policy Manual; State or Federal Statutory Authority.

Policy: The investigator shall conduct a scene "walk through" to establish pertinent scene parameters.

Procedure: Upon arrival at the scene, the investigator should:

A. Reassess scene boundaries and adjust as appropriate.

B. Establish a path of entry and exit.

C. Identify visible physical and fragile evidence.

D. Document and photograph fragile evidence immediately and collect if appropriate.

E. Locate and view the decedent.

Summary:

The initial scene "walk through" is essential to minimize scene disturbance and to prevent the loss and/or contamination of physical and fragile evidence.

6. Establish Chain of Custody

Principle: Ensuring the integrity of the evidence by establishing and maintaining a chain of custody is vital to an investigation. This will safeguard against subsequent allegations of tampering, theft, planting, and contamination of evidence.

Authorization: Medical Examiner/Coroner Official Office Policy Manual; State or Federal Statutory Authority.

Policy: Prior to the removal of any evidence, the custodian(s) of evidence shall be designated and shall generate and maintain a chain of custody for all evidence collected.

Procedure: Throughout the investigation, those responsible for preserving the chain of custody should:

A. Document location of the scene and time of arrival of the death investigator at the scene.

B. Determine custodian(s) of evidence, determine which agency(ies) is/are responsible for collection of specific types of evidence, and determine evidence collection priority for fragile/fleeting evidence.

C. Identify, secure, and preserve evidence with proper containers, labels, and preservatives.

D. Document the collection of evidence by recording its location at the scene, time of collection, and time and location of disposition.

E. Develop personnel lists, witness lists, and documentation of times of arrival and departure of personnel.

Summary:

It is essential to maintain a proper chain of custody for evidence. Through proper documentation, collection, and preservation, the integrity of the evidence can be assured. A properly maintained chain of custody and prompt transfer will reduce the likelihood of a challenge to the integrity of the evidence.

7. Follow Laws (Related to the Collection of Evidence)

Principle: The investigator must follow local, State, and Federal laws for the collection of evidence to ensure its admissibility. The investigator must work with law enforcement and the legal authorities to determine laws regarding collection of evidence.

Authorization: Medical Examiner/Coroner Official Office Policy Manual; State or Federal Statutory Authority.

Policy: The investigator working with other agencies must identify and work under appropriate legal authority. Modification of informal procedures may be necessary but laws must always be followed.

Procedure: The investigator, prior to or upon arrival at the death scene, should work with other agencies to:

A. Determine the need for a search warrant (discuss with appropriate agencies).

B. Identify local, State, Federal, and international laws (discuss with appropriate agencies).

C. Identify medical examiner/coroner statutes and/or office standard operating procedures (discuss with appropriate agencies).

Summary:

Following laws related to the collection of evidence will ensure a complete and proper investigation in compliance with State and local laws, admissibility in court, and adherence to office policies and protocols.

Documenting and Evaluating the Scene

1. Photograph Scene

Principle: The photographic documentation of the scene creates a permanent historical record of the scene. Photographs provide detailed corroborating evidence that constructs a system of redundancy should questions arise concerning the report, witness statements, or position of evidence at the scene.

Authorization: Medical Examiner/Coroner Official Office Policy Manual; State or Federal Statutory Authority.

Policy: The investigator shall obtain detailed photographic documentation of the scene that provides both instant and permanent high-quality (e.g., 35 mm) images.

Procedure: Upon arrival at the scene, and prior to moving the body or evidence, the investigator should:

A. Remove all nonessential personnel from the scene.

B. Obtain an overall (wide-angle) view of the scene to spatially locate the specific scene to the surrounding area.

C. Photograph specific areas of the scene to provide more detailed views of specific areas within the larger scene.

D. Photograph the scene from different angles to provide various perspectives that may uncover additional evidence.

E. Obtain some photographs with scales to document specific evidence.

F. Obtain photographs even if the body or other evidence has been moved.

1. Photograph Scene

Note: If evidence has been moved prior to photography, it should be noted in the report, but the body or other evidence should not be reintroduced into the scene in order to take photographs.

Summary:

Photography allows for the best permanent documentation of the death scene. It is essential that accurate scene photographs are available for other investigators, agencies, and authorities to recreate the scene. Photographs are a permanent record of the terminal event and retain evidentiary value and authenticity. It is essential that the investigator obtain accurate photographs before releasing the scene.

2. Develop Descriptive Documentation of the Scene

Principle: Written documentation of the scene(s) provides a permanent record that may be used to correlate with and enhance photographic documentation, refresh recollections, and record observations.

Authorization: Medical Examiner/Coroner Official Office Policy Manual; State or Federal Statutory Authority.

Policy: Investigators shall provide written scene documentation.

Procedure: After photographic documentation of the scene and prior to removal of the body or other evidence, the investigator should:

A. Diagram/describe in writing items of evidence and their relationship to the body with necessary measurements.

B. Describe and document, with necessary measurements, blood and body fluid evidence including volume, patterns, spatters, and other characteristics.

C. Describe scene environments including odors, lights, temperatures, and other fragile evidence.

Note: If evidence has been moved prior to written documentation, it should be noted in the report.

Summary:

Written scene documentation is essential to correlate with photographic evidence and to recreate the scene for police, forensic(s), and judicial and civil agencies with a legitimate interest.

3. Establish Probable Location of Injury or Illness

Principle: The location where the decedent is found may not be the actual location where the injury/illness that contributed to the death occurred. It is imperative that the investigator attempt to determine the locations of any and all injury(ies)/illness(es) that may have contributed to the death. Physical evidence at any and all locations may be pertinent in establishing the cause, manner, and circumstances of death.

Authorization: Medical Examiner/Coroner Official Office Policy Manual; State or Federal Statutory Authority.

Policy: The investigator shall obtain detailed information regarding any and all probable locations associated with the individual's death.

Procedure: The investigator should:

A. Document location where death was confirmed.

B. Determine location from which decedent was transported and how body was transported to scene.

3. Establish Probable Location of Injury or Illness

C. Identify and record discrepancies in rigor mortis, livor mortis, and body temperature.

D. Check body, clothing, and scene for consistency/inconsistency of trace evidence and indicate location where artifacts are found.

E. Check for drag marks (on body and ground).

F. Establish post-injury activity.

G. Obtain dispatch (e.g., police, ambulance) record(s).

H. Interview family members and associates as needed.

Summary:

Due to post-injury survival, advances in emergency medical services, multiple modes of transportation, the availability of specialized care, or criminal activity, a body may be moved from the actual location of illness/injury to a remote site. It is imperative that the investigator attempt to determine any and all locations where the decedent has previously been and the mode of transport from these sites.

4. Collect, Inventory, and Safeguard Property and Evidence

Principle: The decedent's valuables/property must be safeguarded to ensure proper processing and eventual return to next of kin. Evidence on or near the body must be safeguarded to ensure its availability for further evaluation.

Authorization: Medical Examiner/Coroner Official Office Policy Manual; State or Federal Statutory Authority.

Policy: The investigator shall ensure that all property and evidence is collected, inventoried, safeguarded, and released as required by law.

Procedure: After personal property and evidence have been identified at the scene, the investigator (with a witness) should:

A. Inventory, collect, and safeguard illicit drugs and paraphernalia at scene and/or office.

B. Inventory, collect, and safeguard prescription medication at scene and/or office.

C. Inventory, collect, and safeguard over-the-counter medications at scene and/or office.

D. Inventory, collect, and safeguard money at scene and at office.

E. Inventory, collect, and safeguard personal valuables/property at scene and at office.

Summary:

Personal property and evidence are important items at a death investigation. Evidence must be safeguarded to ensure its availability if needed for future evaluation and litigation. Personal property must be safeguarded to ensure its eventual distribution to appropriate agencies or individuals and to reduce the likelihood that the investigator will be accused of stealing property.

5.   Interview Witness[es] at the Scene

Principle: The documented comments of witnesses at the scene allow the investigator to obtain primary source data regarding discovery of body, witness corroboration, and terminal history. The documented interview provides essential information for the investigative process.

Authorization: Medical Examiner/Coroner Official Office Policy Manual; State or Federal Statutory Authority.

Policy: The investigator's report shall include the source of information, including specific statements and informa-tion provided by the witness.

5. Interview Witness[es] at the Scene

Procedure: Upon arriving at the scene, the investigator should:

A. Collect all available identifying data on witnesses (e.g., full name, address, DOB, work and home telephone numbers, etc.).

B. Establish witness' relationship/association to the deceased.

C. Establish the basis of witness' knowledge (how does witness have knowledge of the death?).

D. Obtain information from each witness.

E. Note discrepancies from the scene briefing (challenge, explain, verify statements).

F. Tape statements where such equipment is available and retain them.

Summary:

The final report must document witness' identity and must include a summary of witness' statements, corroboration with other witnesses, and the circumstances of discovery of the death. This documentation must exist as a permanent record to establish a chain of events.

Documenting and Evaluating the Body

1.   Photograph the Body

Principle: The photographic documentation of the body at the scene creates a permanent record that preserves essential details of the body position, appearance, identity, and final movements. Photographs allow sharing of information with other agencies investigating the death.

Authorization: Medical Examiner/Coroner Official Office Policy Manual; State or Federal Statutory Authority.

Policy: The investigator shall obtain detailed photographic documentation of the body that provides both instant and permanent high-quality (e.g., 35 mm) images.

Procedure: Upon arrival at the scene, and prior to moving the body or evidence, the investigator should:

A. Photograph the body and immediate scene (including the decedent as initially found).

B. Photograph the decedent's face.

C. Take additional photographs after removal of objects/items that interfere with photographic documentation of the decedent (e.g., body removed from car).

D. Photograph the decedent with and without measurements (as appropriate).

E. Photograph the surface beneath the body (after the body has been removed, as appropriate).

Note: Never clean face, do not change condition. Take multiple shots if possible.

D

1. Photograph the Body

Summary:

The photographic documentation of the body at the scene provides for documentation of the body position, identity, and appearance. The details of the body at the scene provide investigators with pertinent information of the terminal events.

2. Conduct External Body Examination (Superficial)

Principle: Conducting the external body examination provides the investigator with objective data regarding the single most important piece of evidence at the scene, the body. This documentation provides detailed information regarding the decedent's physical attributes, his/her relationship to the scene, and possible cause, manner, and circumstances of death.

Authorization: Medical Examiner/Coroner Official Office Policy Manual; State or Federal Statutory Authority.

Policy: The investigator shall obtain detailed photographs and written documentation of the decedent at the scene.

Procedure: After arrival at the scene and prior to moving the decedent, the investigator should, without removing decedent's clothing:

A. Photograph the scene, including the decedent as initially found and the surface beneath the body after the body has been removed.

   Note: If necessary, take additional photographs after removal of objects/items that interfere with photographic documentation of the decedent.

B. Photograph the decedent with and without measurements (as appropriate), including a photograph of the decedent's face.

C. Document the decedent's position with and without measurements (as appropriate).

D. Document the decedent's physical characteristics.

E. Document the presence or absence of clothing and personal effects.

F. Document the presence or absence of any items/objects that may be relevant.

G. Document the presence or absence of marks, scars, and tattoos.

H. Document the presence or absence of injury/trauma, petechiae, etc.

I. Document the presence of treatment or resuscitative efforts.

J. Based on the findings, determine the need for further evaluation/ assistance of forensic specialists (e.g., pathologists, odontologists).

Summary:

Thorough evaluation and documentation (photographic and written) of the deceased at the scene is essential to determine the depth and direction the investigation will take.

3. Preserve Evidence (on Body)

Principle: The photographic and written documentation of evidence on the body allows the investigator to obtain a permanent historical record of that evidence. To maintain chain of custody, evidence must be collected, preserved, and transported properly. In addition to all of the physical evidence visible on the body, blood and other body fluids present must be photographed and documented prior to collection and transport. Fragile evidence (that which can be easily contaminated, lost, or altered) must also be collected and/or preserved to maintain chain of custody and to assist in determination of cause, manner, and circumstances of death.

3. Preserve Evidence (on Body)

Authorization: Medical Examiner/Coroner Official Office Policy
Manual; State or Federal Statutory Authority.

Policy: With photographic and written documentation, the
investigator will provide a permanent record of evidence
that is on the body.

Procedure: Once evidence on the body is recognized, the
investigator should:

A. Photograph the evidence.

B. Document blood/body fluid on the body (froth/purge, substances
from orifices), location, and pattern before transporting.

C. Place decedent's hands and/or feet in unused paper bags (as
determined by the scene).

D. Collect trace evidence before transporting the body (e.g., blood,
hair, fibers, etc.).

E. Arrange for the collection and transport of evidence at the scene
(when necessary).

F. Ensure the proper collection of blood and body fluids for subsequent analysis (if body will be released from scene to an outside
agency without an autopsy).

Summary:

It is essential that evidence be collected, preserved, transported,
and documented in an orderly and proper fashion to ensure the chain of
custody and admissibility in a legal action. The preservation and documentation of the evidence on the body must be initiated by the investigator at the scene to prevent alterations or contamination.

4. Establish Decedent Identification

Principle: The establishment or confirmation of the decedent's identity is paramount to the death investigation. Proper identification allows notification of next of kin, settlement of estates, resolution of criminal and civil litigation, and the proper completion of the death certificate.

Authorization: Medical Examiner/Coroner Official Office Policy Manual; State or Federal Statutory Authority.

Policy: The investigator shall engage in a diligent effort to establish/confirm the decedent's identity.

Procedure: To establish identity, the investigator should document use of the following methods:

A. Direct visual or photographic identification of the decedent if visually recognizable.

B. Scientific methods such as fingerprints, dental, radiographic, and DNA comparisons.

C. Circumstantial methods such as (but not restricted to) personal effects, circumstances, physical characteristics, tattoos, and anthropologic data.

Summary:

There are several methods available that can be used to properly identify deceased persons. This is essential for investigative, judicial, family, and vital records issues.

5. Document Post Mortem Changes

Principle: The documenting of post mortem changes to the body assists the investigator in explaining body appearance in the interval following death. Inconsistencies between post

5. Document Post Mortem Changes

mortem changes and body location may indicate movement of body and validate or invalidate witness statements. In addition, post mortem changes to the body, when correlated with circumstantial information, can assist the investigators in estimating the approximate time of death.

Authorization: Medical Examiner/Coroner Official Office Policy Manual; State or Federal Statutory Authority.

Policy: The investigator shall document all post mortem changes relative to the decedent and the environment.

Procedure: Upon arrival at the scene and prior to moving the body, the investigator should note the presence of each of the following in his/her report:

A. Livor (color, location, blanchability, Tardieu spots) consistent/inconsistent with position of the body.

B. Rigor (stage/intensity, location on the body, broken, inconsistent with the scene).

C. Degree of decomposition (putrefaction, adipocere, mummification, skeletonization, as appropriate).

D. Insect and animal activity.

E. Scene temperature (document method used and time estimated).

F. Description of body temperature (e.g., warm, cold, frozen) or measurement of body temperature (document method used and time of measurement).

Summary:

Documentation of post mortem changes in every report is essential to determine an accurate cause and manner of death, provide information as to the time of death, corroborate witness statements, and indicate that the body may have been moved after death.

6.   Participate in Scene Debriefing

Principle: The scene debriefing helps investigators from all participating agencies to establish post-scene responsibilities by sharing data regarding particular scene findings. The scene debriefing provides each agency the opportunity for input regarding special requests for assistance, additional information, special examinations, and other requests requiring interagency communication, cooperation, and education.

Authorization: Medical Examiner/Coroner Official Office Policy Manual; State or Federal Statutory Authority.

Policy: The investigator shall participate in or initiate interagency scene debriefing to verify specific post-scene responsibilities.

Procedure: When participating in scene debriefing, the investigator should:

A. Determine post-scene responsibilities (identification, notification, press relations, and evidence transportation).

B. Determine/identify the need for a specialist (e.g., crime laboratory technicians, social services, entomologists, OSHA).

C. Communicate with the pathologist about responding to the scene or to the autopsy schedule (as needed).

D. Share investigative data (as required in furtherance of the investigation).

E. Communicate special requests to appropriate agencies, being mindful of the necessity for confidentiality.

Summary:

The scene debriefing is the best opportunity for investigative participants to communicate special requests and confirm all current and additional scene responsibilities. The debriefing allows participants the opportunity to establish clear lines of responsibility for a successful investigation.

7. Determine Notification Procedures (Next of Kin)

Principle: Every reasonable effort should be made to notify the next of kin as soon as possible. Notification of next of kin initiates closure for the family, disposition of remains, and facilitates the collection of additional information relative to the case.

Authorization: Medical Examiner/Coroner Official Office Policy Manual; State or Federal Statutory Authority.

Policy: The investigator shall ensure that next of kin is notified of the death and that all failed and successful attempts at notification are documented.

Procedure: When determining notification procedures, the investigator should:

A. Identify next of kin (determine who will perform task).

B. Locate next of kin (determine who will perform task).

C. Notify next of kin (assign person(s) to perform task) and record time of notification, or, if delegated to another agency, gain confirmation when notification is made.

D. Notify concerned agencies of status of the notification.

Summary:

The investigator is responsible for ensuring that the next of kin is identified, located, and notified in a timely manner. The time and method of notification should be documented. Failure to locate next of kin and efforts to do so should be a matter of record. This ensures that every reasonable effort has been made to contact the family.

8. Ensure Security of Remains

Principle: Ensuring security of the body requires the investigator to supervise the labeling, packaging, and removal of the remains. An appropriate identification tag is placed on the body to preclude misidentification upon receipt at the examining agency. This function also includes safeguarding all potential physical evidence and/or property and clothing that remain on the body.

Authorization: Medical Examiner/Coroner Official Office Policy Manual; State or Federal Statutory Authority.

Policy: The investigator shall supervise and ensure the proper identification, inventory, and security of evidence/property and its packaging and removal from the scene.

Procedure: Prior to leaving the scene, the investigator should:

A. Ensure that the body is protected from further trauma or contamination (if not, document) and unauthorized removal of therapeutic and resuscitative equipment.

B. Inventory and secure property, clothing, and personal effects that are on the body (remove in a controlled environment with witness present).

C. Identify property and clothing to be retained as evidence (in a controlled environment).

D. Recover blood and/or vitreous samples prior to release of remains.

E. Place identification on the body and body bag.

F. Ensure/supervise the placement of the body into the bag.

G. Ensure/supervise the removal of the body from the scene.

H. Secure transportation.

8. Ensure Security of Remains

Summary:

Ensuring the security of the remains facilitates proper identification of the remains, maintains a proper chain of custody, and safeguards property and evidence.

1. Document the Discovery History

Principle: Establishing a decedent profile includes documenting a discovery history and circumstances surrounding the discovery. The basic profile will dictate subsequent levels of investigation, jurisdiction, and authority. The focus (breadth/depth) of further investigation is dependent on this information.

Authorization: Medical Examiner/Coroner Official Office Policy Manual; State or Federal Statutory Authority.

Policy: The investigator shall document the discovery history, available witnesses, and apparent circumstances leading to death.

Procedure: For an investigator to correctly document the discovery history, he/she should:

A. Establish and record person(s) who discovered the body and when.

B. Document the circumstances surrounding the discovery (who, what, where, when, how).

E

Summary:

The investigator must produce clear, concise, documented information concerning who discovered the body, what are the circumstances of discovery, where the discovery occurred, when the discovery was made, and how the discovery was made.

2. Determine Terminal Episode History

Principle: Pre-terminal circumstances play a significant role in determining cause and manner of death. Documentation of medical intervention and/or procurement of ante mortem specimens help to establish the decedent's condition prior to death.

Authorization: Medical Examiner/Coroner Official Office Policy Manual; State or Federal Statutory Authority.

Policy: The investigator shall document known circumstances and medical intervention preceding death.

Procedure: In order for the investigator to determine terminal episode history, he/she should:

A. Document when, where, how, and by whom decedent was last known to be alive.

B. Document the incidents prior to the death.

C. Document complaints/symptoms prior to the death.

D. Document and review complete EMS records (including the initial electrocardiogram).

E. Obtain relevant medical records (copies).

F. Obtain relevant ante mortem specimens.

Summary:

Obtaining records of pre-terminal circumstances and medical history distinguishes medical treatment from trauma. This history and relevant ante mortem specimens assist the medical examiner/coroner in determining cause and manner of death.

3.   Document Decedent Medical History

Principle: The majority of deaths referred to the medical examiner/ coroner are natural deaths. Establishing the decedent's medical history helps to focus the investigation. Documenting the decedent's medical signs or symptoms prior to death determines the need for subsequent examinations. The relationship between disease and injury may play a role in the cause, manner, and circumstances of death.

Authorization: Medical Examiner/Coroner Official Office Policy Manual; State or Federal Statutory Authority.

Policy: The investigator shall obtain the decedent's past medical history.

Procedure: Through interviews and review of the written records, the investigator should:

A. Document medical history, including medications taken, alcohol and drug use, and family medical history from family members and witnesses.

B. Document information from treating physicians and/or hospitals to confirm history and treatment.

C. Document physical characteristics and traits (e.g., left-/right-handedness, missing appendages, tattoos, etc.).

Summary:

Obtaining a thorough medical history focuses the investigation, aids in disposition of the case, and helps determine the need for a post mortem examination or other laboratory tests or studies.

4. Document Decedent Mental Health History

Principle: The decedent's mental health history can provide insight into the behavior/state of mind of the individual. That insight may produce clues that will aid in establishing the cause, manner, and circumstances of the death.

Authorization: Medical Examiner/Coroner Official Office Policy Manual; State or Federal Statutory Authority.

Policy: The investigator shall obtain information from sources familiar with the decedent pertaining to the decedent's mental health history.

Procedure: The investigator should:

A. Document the decedent's mental health history, including hospitalizations and medications.

B. Document the history of suicidal ideations, gestures, and/or attempts.

C. Document mental health professionals (e.g., psychiatrists, psychologists, counselors, etc.) who treated the decedent.

D. Document family mental health history.

Summary:

Knowledge of the mental health history allows the investigator to evaluate properly the decedent's state of mind and contributes to the determination of cause, manner, and circumstances of death.

5. Document Social History

Principle: Social history includes marital, family, sexual, educational, employment, and financial information. Daily routines, habits and activities, and friends and associates of the decedent help in developing the decedent's profile. This information will aid in establishing the cause, manner, and circumstances of death.

Authorization: Medical Examiner/Coroner Official Office Policy Manual; State or Federal Statutory Authority.

Policy: The investigator shall obtain social history information from sources familiar with the decedent.

Procedure: When collecting relevant social history information, the investigator should:

A. Document marital/domestic history.

B. Document family history (similar deaths, significant dates).

C. Document sexual history.

D. Document employment history.

E. Document financial history.

F. Document daily routines, habits, and activities.

G. Document relationships, friends, and associates.

H. Document religious, ethnic, or other pertinent information (e.g., religious objection to autopsy).

I. Document educational background.

J. Document criminal history.

Summary:

Information from sources familiar with the decedent pertaining to the decedent's social history assists in determining cause, manner, and circumstances of death.

Completing the Scene Investigation

1.   Maintain Jurisdiction Over the Body

Principle: Maintaining jurisdiction over the body allows the investigator to protect the chain of custody as the body is transported from the scene for autopsy, specimen collection, or storage.

Authorization: Medical Examiner/Coroner Official Office Policy Manual; State or Federal Statutory Authority.

Policy: The investigator shall maintain jurisdiction of the body by arranging for the body to be transported for autopsy, specimen collection, or storage by secure conveyance.

Procedure: When maintaining jurisdiction over the body, the investigator should:

A.   Arrange for, and document, secure transportation of the body to a medical or autopsy facility for further examination or storage.

B.   Coordinate and document procedures to be performed when the body is received at the facility.

Summary:

By providing documented secure transportation of the body from the scene to an authorized receiving facility, the investigator maintains jurisdiction and protects chain of custody of the body.

F

2. Release Jurisdiction of the Body

Principle: Prior to releasing jurisdiction of the body to an authorized receiving agent or funeral director, it is necessary to determine the person responsible for certification of the death. Information to complete the death certificate includes demographic information and the date, time, and location of death.

Authorization: Medical Examiner/Coroner Official Office Policy Manual; State or Federal Statutory Authority.

Policy: The investigator shall obtain sufficient data to enable completion of the death certificate and release of jurisdiction over the body.

Procedure: When releasing jurisdiction over the body, the investigator should:

A. Determine who will sign the death certificate (name, agency, etc.).

B. Confirm the date, time, and location of death.

C. Collect, when appropriate, blood, vitreous fluid, and other evidence prior to release of the body from the scene.

D. Document and arrange with the authorized receiving agent to reconcile all death certificate information.

E. Release the body to a funeral director or other authorized receiving agent.

Summary:

The investigator releases jurisdiction only after determining who will sign the death certificate; documenting the date, time, and location of death; collecting appropriate specimens; and releasing the body to the funeral director or other authorized receiving agent.

3.   Perform Exit Procedures

Principle: Bringing closure to the scene investigation ensures that important evidence has been collected and the scene has been processed. In addition, a systematic review of the scene ensures that artifacts or equipment are not inadvertently left behind (e.g., used disposable gloves, paramedical debris, film wrappers, etc.), and any dangerous materials or conditions have been reported.

Authorization: Medical Examiner/Coroner Official Office Policy Manual; State or Federal Statutory Authority.

Policy: At the conclusion of the scene investigation, the investigator shall conduct a post-investigative "walk through" and ensure the scene investigation is complete.

Procedure: When performing exit procedures, the investigator should:

A. Identify, inventory, and remove all evidence collected at the scene.

B. Remove all personal equipment and materials from the scene.

C. Report and document any dangerous materials or conditions.

Summary:

Conducting a scene "walk through" upon exit ensures that all evidence has been collected, that materials are not inadvertently left behind, and that any dangerous materials or conditions have been reported to the proper entities.

4.   Assist the Family

Principle: The investigator provides the family with a timetable so they can arrange for final disposition and provides information on available community and professional resources that may assist the family.

Authorization: Medical Examiner/Coroner Official Office Policy Manual; State or Federal Statutory Authority.

Policy: The investigator shall offer the decedent's family information regarding available community and professional resources.

Procedure: When the investigator is assisting the family, it is important to:

A. Inform the family if an autopsy is required.

B. Inform the family of available support services (e.g., victim assistance, police, social services, etc.).

C. Inform the family of appropriate agencies to contact with questions (medical examiner/coroner offices, law enforcement, SIDS support group, etc.).

D. Ensure family is not left alone with body (if circumstances warrant).

E. Inform the family of approximate body release timetable.

F. Inform the family of information release timetable (toxicology, autopsy results, etc., as required).

G. Inform the family of available reports, including cost, if any.

Summary:

The interaction with the family allows the investigator to assist and direct them to appropriate resources. It is essential that families be given a timetable of events so that they can make necessary arrangements. In addition, the investigator needs to make them aware of what and when information will be available.

About the National Institute of Justice

The National Institute of Justice (NIJ), a component of the Office of Justice Programs, is the research agency of the U.S. Department of Justice. Created by the Omnibus Crime Control and Safe Streets Act of 1968, as amended, NIJ is authorized to support research, evaluation, and demonstration programs, development of technology, and both national and international information dissemination. Specific mandates of the Act direct NIJ to:

◆ Sponsor special projects, and research and development programs, that will improve and strengthen the criminal justice system and reduce or prevent crime.

◆ Conduct national demonstration projects that employ innovative or promising approaches for improving criminal justice.

◆ Develop new technologies to fight crime and improve criminal justice.

◆ Evaluate the effectiveness of criminal justice programs and identify programs that promise to be successful if continued or repeated.

◆ Recommend actions that can be taken by Federal, State, and local governments as well as by private organizations to improve criminal justice.

◆ Carry out research on criminal behavior.

◆ Develop new methods of crime prevention and reduction of crime and delinquency.

In recent years, NIJ has greatly expanded its initiatives, the result of the Violent Crime Control and Law Enforcement Act of 1994 (the Crime Act), partnerships with other Federal agencies and private foundations, advances in technology, and a new international focus. Some examples of these new initiatives:

◆ New research and evaluation is exploring key issues in community policing, violence against women, sentencing reforms, and specialized courts such as drug courts.

◆ Dual-use technologies are being developed to support national defense and local law enforcement needs.

◆ Four regional National Law Enforcement and Corrections Technology Centers and a Border Research and Technology Center have joined the National Center in Rockville, Maryland.

◆ The causes, treatment, and prevention of violence against women and violence within the family are being investigated in cooperation with several agencies of the U.S. Department of Health and Human Services.

◆ NIJ's links with the international community are being strengthened through membership in the United Nations network of criminological institutes; participation in developing the U.N. Criminal Justice Information Network; initiation of UNOJUST (U.N. Online Justice Clearinghouse), which electronically links the institutes to the U.N. network; and establishment of an NIJ International Center.

◆ The NIJ-administered criminal justice information clearinghouse, the world's largest, has improved its online capability.

◆ The Institute's Drug Use Forecasting (DUF) program has been expanded and enhanced. Renamed ADAM (Arrestee Drug Abuse Monitoring), the program will increase the number of drug-testing sites, and its role as a "platform" for studying drug-related crime will grow.

◆ NIJ's new Crime Mapping Research Center will provide training in computer mapping technology, collect and archive geocoded crime data, and develop analytic software.

◆ The Institute's program of intramural research has been expanded and enhanced.

The Institute Director, who is appointed by the President and confirmed by the Senate, establishes the Institute's objectives, guided by the priorities of the Office of Justice Programs, the Department of Justice, and the needs of the criminal justice field. The Institute actively solicits the views of criminal justice professionals and researchers in the continuing search for answers that inform public policymaking in crime and justice.

For information on the National Institute of Justice, please contact:

National Criminal Justice Reference Service
Box 6000
Rockville, MD 20849–6000
800–851–3420
e-mail: askncjrs@ncjrs.org

You can view or obtain an electronic version of this document from the
NCJRS Justice Information Center World Wide Web site.
To access this site, go to http://www.ncjrs.org

If you have questions, call or e-mail NCJRS.

Made in the USA
Lexington, KY
18 June 2017